Dear readers,

Thanks so much for reading this edition of Outhouse Books. In this edition, we present unique facts, trivia, lore, and games related to the most wonderful time of the year, Christmas.

Hopefully you enjoy this brand of specialized reader. It is designed for those of you who like to have a sense of accomplishment, but have limited time to read. These quick readers can be completed in one session....even in the privacy of your own "outhouse."

We hope you enjoy! Happy reading!!!

Sincerely,
The Outhouse Staff

Want to read about the birth of
Jesus. It is only found in the gospels
of Mark and Luke.

The first Christmas card was sent in the mid 1800s. A man named Sir Henry Cole was too busy to send his Christmas letter. So he had a renown painter, John Callcott Horsley design a card to send to friends. It had a simple message – "A Merry Christmas and a Happy New Year To You." Since that day, the custom of sending Christmas cards has stuck.

The first fake Christmas trees were made of feathers and invented in Germany in the mid 1800s.

It is believed that St. Francis of Assisi developed the first Nativity scene in 1223. It consisted of a doll of the Christ child placed on an altar of stones with a real ox and donkey around it.

In the 1960s, aluminum Christmas trees with revolving lights on the bottom were a fad. These trees went out of fashion in the 1970s. So, the next time you watch *A Charlie Brown Christmas* and Linus and Lucy talk about aluminum Christmas trees, they are sharing the fad of the day.

The National Christmas Tree Association gives the U.S. president a Christmas tree each year. It began the tradition in 1966.

Turkey anyone? In America, 22 million turkeys are the main course of dinner at Christmas (that is about half of the 45 million that are meals at Thanksgiving).

It happened on Christmas Eve...

On December 24, 1814, the War of 1812 came to an end. Unfortunately the last, and most famous battle (The Battle of New Orleans) happened about a month later, because it took so long for the news to reach America.

"O Come All Ye Faithful" is a classic Christmas carol originally written in Latin. The original title is "Hymn for Christmas Day."

The Salvation Army helps nearly six million people every year.

Tradition has it....

In the southern parts of the United States, people used to leave a loaf of bread on the table following Christmas dinner. This was meant to ensure they had all the "bread" they needed in the year ahead.

It actually is not anti-Christmas to say "Merry X-Mas." The phrase comes from ancient Greek. The first letter in the word Christ is "chi," which is the same letter as "X" in the Latin alphabet. Hence Merry X-Mas to you.

In Jesus's day, a stable was in a cave or made of stone. That is why many religious mangers are found designed in a cave.

Christmas Island can be found in the Pacific Ocean.

There are more than three billion
Christmas cards sent out each year.

In 1809, Washington Irving helped provide the first American description of Santa Claus. In his book *A History of New York*, the kindly gift giver, who appears to be a more svelte man, is described and even illustrated.

It's a hit...

The hit toy in America in 1867. Well,
according to the Toy Industry
Association, it was none other than the
official board game of India,
Parcheesi®.

Five Christmas Quotes to Live By:

1. Christmas is not a time or a season but a state of mind. To cherish peace and good will, to be plenteous in mercy, is to have the real spirit of Christmas.
> - Calvin Coolidge

2. Christmas is doing a little something extra for someone.
> - Charles Schulz

3. I will honor Christmas in my heart and try to keep it all the year."
> -Ebenezer Scrooge (in Charles Dickens' *A Christmas Carol*)

4. It is not even the beginning of Christmas unless it is Christmas in the heart.
> - Richard Roberts (in *Contemporary Christ*)

5. Christmas gift suggestions: to your enemy, forgiveness. To an opponent, tolerance. To a friend, your heart. To a customer, service. To all, charity. To every child, a good example. To yourself, respect.
> - Oren Arnold

Tradition has it...

Long ago, the people in Sweden often stayed inside houses during Christmas Eve. Ancient Swedes believed that trolls roamed the land on this night, disappearing on Christmas morning. 'Twas best to lay low.

In 1922, Clement Clark Moore wrote *A Vist From Saint Nicolas* (better known as 'Twas the Night Before Christmas*) as a Christmas poem and gift for his children. This poem created the current impression of Santa, depicting him as a jolly, and more "round," fellow.

The altar located inside the Church of the Nativity in Bethlehem is believed to be the actual site where Jesus was born.

Christmas trees can remove dust and pollen from the air, but they can also share allergens as well.

Gingerbread is not just for Christmas cookies and houses. Years ago, in England, woman used it as the ultimate husband finder. It was believed by eating gingerbread, woman would have help finding a husband. No one knows what the prospective husbands had to eat to find their wives.

People from Scandinavian cultures used to burn Yule logs around the winter solstice. It was a way to honor the return of the sun...and ward off evil spirits.

Before the 1500s, it was common for people to give other people presents on December 6th, the feast of St. Nicholas. The real St. Nick was a Turkish bishop for gave gifts to the poor in the fourth century.

It's a hit....

Perhaps you have seen *The Christmas Story* where the Red Rider BB gun was the must have gift of the time (around 1940). Well, according to the Toy Industry Association, the popular gift of that time – around 1939 – was the View Master 3D® viewer.

Wishing you a Feliz Navidad. Here are ten other ways to say Merry Christmas from around the world.

Arabia: Milad Majid
China (Mandarin dialect): Sheng Dan Kuai Le
Inuit: Jutdlime pivdluarit ukiortame pivdluaritlo
Manx: Nollick ghennal as blein vie noa
Navajo: Merry Keshmish
Netherland: Vrolijk Kerstfeest en enn Gelukkig Nieuwjaar
Portugal: Feliz Natal
Sweden: Good Jul and Ett Gott Nyatt Ar
Thailand: Sawadee Pee Mai
Vietnam: Chuc Mung Giang Sinh

Lucky mushrooms? Many people in Germany think so. Traditionalists in Germany hang mushroom ornaments to promote good luck in the New Year.

AKA Santa. In Holland the jolly fellow is known as Sinter Klaas. In France, he is called Père Nöel. And in England, he is called Father Christmas.

Wassail is an actual drink. Popular in medieval times, the drink consisted of ale, hard cider, or wine topped with stale bread (yum!) or eggs that have been whipped. Travelers roamed door to door with a wassail bowl, visiting neighbors on Christmas Eve. They would drink the wassail (which is an Old Norse word for "in good health") to salute their health.

Charlie Brown Christmas Quiz

See how well you know these questions to the classic Christmas story, A *Charlie Brown Christmas*. Answers follow on the next page...

1. Based on his discussion with Lucy, Charlie Brown declares he has this phobia?

2. What animals did Snoopy pretend to be for the Christmas play?

3. What type of trees did Lucy and her friends think Charlie Brown should get?

4. What type of music was Schroeder trying to specialize in while talking to Lucy?

5. Charlie Brown puts this color ornament on the tree.

6. What place did Snoopy come in while participating in the neighborhood lights and display contest?

7. What song did the Peanuts gang sing at the end of the TV special?

Charlie Brown Quiz answers...

1. pentaphobia....the fear of everything

2. cow, sheep, penguin, vulture

3. "a great big, shiny, aluminum tree....perhaps painted pink"

4. Beethoven Christmas music

5. red

6. first place

7. Hark the Herald Angels Sing

The first candy canes were made straight and without stripes. A choir director in Cologne, Germany later made them into a bent shape in the 1600s to resemble the shape of a shepherd's hook. His design helped to keep kids quiet while waiting to sing at church. The beloved treat didn't get its legendary striped design until the 1900s.

During World War II America cut back on electricity use. As a result, the famous Rockefeller Center Christmas Tree was not lit.

Tradition has it...

Fisherman from Scotland pour ale into the ocean around Christmastime each year. This is done in the hopes of providing a healthy catch in the year ahead.

The Christ Child is believed to be the gift giver on Christmas in the country of Guatemala.

God Bless Us Everyone. Before deciding to name his little protagonist Tiny Tim, Charles Dickens bandied a few other monikers. Among them were Little Larry, Puny Pete, and Small Sam.

Greeks burn a large log – called a *skarkantzalos* – for 12 days.

Christmas Island: Fact or Fiction

Look at these five statements about Christmas Island. Check if they are fact or fiction.

1. The official name of the island is The island of Christmas.

    FACT ☐   FICTION ☐

2. The island was discovered on Christmas Day in 1643.

    FACT ☐   FICTION ☐

3. More than half the island is actually a national park.

    FACT ☐   FICTION ☐

4. Geographically speaking, the island is part of Asia.

    FACT ☐   FICTION ☐

5. The official head of state for the island is the king or queen of England.

    FACT ☐   FICTION ☐

Answers to Christmas Island Quiz

1. Fiction. Its real name is Christmas Island.

2. Fact. It was settled by United Kingdom settlers in 1888.

3. Fact

4. Fiction. It is actually part of Australia.

5. Fact. The British monarch is the head of state.

German Protestants popularized the celebration of Christmas on December 25th. They celebrated *Christkindl*, the feast of the *Christ Child*.

Five Facts About Reindeer

1. Reindeer live in the northern parts of Asia, Europe, and America.

2. Reindeer have been used by the Lapps in Norway and the Chukchi and Tungus of Siberia as a source of cheese, butter, and milk.

3. Reindeer are trained to pull sleds.

4. In North America, reindeer are called caribou.

5. The main food of a reindeer is a special type of lichen that grows on the tundra. It is often called "reindeer moss."

Santons are French clay figures. They are made regularly on Christmas.

Name that song. Many Christmas songs are easily recognized by their opening words. However, do you know the second verses? Which Christmas song has a second verse that starts with the following words?

1. Christ by highest heav'n adored.

2. Still through the cloven skies they come,

3. In Bethlehem, in Israel,

4. Hither, page, and stand by me

5. They looked up and saw a star

6. Led by the light of faith serenely beaming,

7. The cattle are lowing

Answers are on the following page...

Answers....how did you do???

1. Hark the Herald Angels Sing

2. It Came Upon A Midnight Clear

3. God Rest Ye Merry Gentlemen

4. Good King Wenceslas

5. The First Noel

6. Oh Holy Night

7. Away in a Manger

In Syria, Santa Claus gives way to the Three Wise Men. They deliver gifts with the help of their camels. The smallest of the camels helps carry the gifts.

Sugarplums may dance in people's heads, but they actually are a food that has changed over time. Originally, they were sweetened seeds popular in the 17th century. By the 18th century, they turned to sugar coated raisins or currants, and a century later, they were hardened sugar candy.

In the movie, *The Christmas Story*, the pole that Flick got stuck to had a device that sucked in air. It gave the illusion that Flick had his tongue stuck to the icy pole.

Check out these Santa Jokes.

1. Why did Santa get a ticket on Christmas Eve?

2. Where does Santa pack his suit after returning home?

3. What are Santa's favorite movies?

4. Why is Santa always so dependable?

5. Why was the squirrel upset with Santa?

6. What is Santa's favorite music?

7. What does Santa say to sheep?

Answers follow...

Joke answers...

1. He left his sleigh in a snow parking zone.

2. In a claus-et

3. Saint Nick Flicks

4. Because he arrives in the "Nick" of time

5. Santa gave him "nut" thin

6. The North "Polka"

7. Season's Bleatings!

The official flower of Christmas – in Costa Rica – is the orchid.

Mincemeat became a Christmas tradition in the 1500s. People believed that eating a pie during the 12 days of Christmas would assure a good year ahead. Mincemeats proved popular because you could help preserve meat from going bad quickly by wrapping it with spices.

Tradition has it...

Oranges are often a staple of
Christmas stockings. But, it is more
than just the fact that oranges fill in
the bottom of tradition stockings
rather nicely. Oranges were considered
exotic fruits only worthy of the rich
about 100 years ago. To get an orange
was truly a "special thing."

Fruitcakes served as a traditional food and gift in years past. While most people scoff at the idea of exchanging fruitcakes for gifts, you occasionally hear rumors about people "re-gifting" fruitcakes. And there is good reason. A fruitcake can actually last 25 years before going bad.

Christmas in America

Check out these city names with a holiday connection.

1. Christmas (in Arizona, Florida, Kentucky, Michigan, and Mississippi)

2. Santa (in Idaho)

3. North Pole (in Alaska, Idaho, New York, and Oklahoma)

4. Humbug (in Arizona)

5. Elf (in North Carolina)

6. Silver Bells (in Arizona)

7. Reindeer (in Missouri)

8. Dasher (in Georgia)

9. Vixen (in Louisiana)

10. Blitzen (in Oregon)

Fa, la, la, la, la. The first Christmas carols were invented to tell the stories of the nativity to people who could not read.

Once Upon A Christmas...

In 1926, Hirohito became Japanese
Emperor on Christmas Day.

Rudolph the Red Nose TV special
Reindeer Quiz

See how well you can answer these questions. Answers are on the following page:

1. What was the name of the jack-in-the box on the TV special?

2. Who was Clarice?

3. Rudolph was the son of this reindeer?

4. What did Hermey hope to do when he grew up?

5. Who was the narrator snowman of the story?

Rudolph answers

1. Charlie

2. Rudolph's doe friend

3. Donder

4. a dentist

5. Sam the snowman

Holly days. Holly was originally used during the Roman festival of Saturnalia that happened during the winter solstice. It was exchanged between people as a way to express friendship. From that time, it has been a part of the holiday season.

Joy to the World was originally written by Isaac Watts in 1719. Watts, who wrote more than 600 songs, became famous for this song because of an American composer named Lowell Mason. Mason put Watt's song to music in 1839, becoming the beloved tune we hear today. Incidentally, Mason may have actually borrowed the tune from Handel of *The Messiah* fame.

Get jumbled:

How many words can you make from
the word CHRISTMAS

Examples: Mast, Chat

_____   _____

_____   _____

_____   _____

_____   _____

_____   _____

_____   _____

_____   _____

_____   _____

Bundle Up. The average temperature of the North Pole is below freezing. No wonder why Santa dresses so warm.

America's National Christmas Tree is not the one in Washington D.C. It is a giant Sequoia better known as the General Grant tree. Located in Sanger, California, it was dubbed the "Nation's Christmas Tree" in 1925.

In 324 AD, by declaration of Constantinople, Christmas was declared a legal holiday in Rome. That meant people could celebrate it without fear of repercussions such as death.

"Silver Bells," written by Richard Evans and Jay Livingston, was originally known as Tinkle Bells...that is until Jay's wife explained that "tinkle" was a slang term for taking a pee. Soon, it was out with the tinkle and in with the silver.

The first Christmas trees were sold in the United States in 1851.

Tradition has it that, at midnight on Christmas Eve (as it turns to Christmas day), animals turn toward Bethlehem and can talk. What do they talk about? Well, no one can hear them, but supposedly they talk about the true meaning of Christmas.

Five Christmas Specials to see every Christmas

1. A Charlie Brown Christmas

2. How the Grinch Stole Christmas

3. Rudolph the Red Nose Reindeer

4. Frosty the Snowman

5. 'Twas the Night Before Christmas (a lost Rankin Bass classic)

Poinsettias account for nearly 90 percent of all Christmas plant purchases. They originated in Mexico, where they are called "Flower of the Holy Night." Ambassador Joel Poinset brought the first ones from Mexico to the US in 1829. Since then, they've become a part of the Christmas scene.

Ancient Druids probably invented the first wreath out of holly. The magical evergreen helped represent eternal life to the ancient Druids. They believed a circle, with no beginning and no end, was a symbol of everlasting life.

What was the first state to declare Christmas a legal holiday? Alabama...in 1836.

Edward Johnson, an assistant to Thomas Edison, invented Christmas lights in 1882. He put 80 red, white, and blue lights on the Christmas tree in his house. It became a hit. Later, the company he worked for, Edison General Electric Co., sold similar lights to the public.

In 1610, tinsel became popular to use on Christmas trees. The silver looked lovely but had a drawback. It tarnished quickly in front of the candlelight. So, lead and tin were used, but proved unwieldy. By the 1900s, aluminum and then plastic took over for the beloved tree decoration.

During the 1600s, when strict Puritans laws ruled the city, it was illegal to celebrate Christmas in the colony of Massachusetts.

The idea of the Christmas tree may actually come from the story of Adam and Eve. In the Middle Ages, travelers performed Christmas plays during the advent season that depicted scenes from the Bible. These included scenes with Adam and Eve near a paradise tree decorated with apples.

Martin Luther, the protestant reformer, is believed to have added lights to Christmas trees. His inspiration came from walking in the woods and seeing starlight twinkle through evergreen branches. There was one problem with his design– his first lights were actually lit candles placed on the tree branches.

Christmas became a Christian holiday in the 4th century. Prior to that time, Christians mainly celebrated Easter. They considered celebrating the birth of gods to be a pagan practice. However, in order to covert pagans more easily, Christian leaders adopted the practice of celebrating the birth of God's son and moved it to a time when the "birth of the sun" was popular with pagans. This is why it is near the winter solstice.

Christmas Timeline:

336: Christmas is celebrated in Rome

1066: William the Conqueror becomes king of England

1776: George Washington crosses the Delaware

1896: Jon Philip Souza writes *The Stars and Stripes Forever*

1950: Walt Disney makes his television debut on NBC.

1914: The famous Christmas Truce between German, Russian, French, and British soldiers occurs in France during WW I.

Thank Grant for Christmas. That's right. In the U.S., you can thank Ulysses S. Grant for making Christmas a holiday. He declared it legal in 1870.

Tradition has it...

In Sweden, it is customary for the oldest daughter to wake up and serenade her parents with the song "Saint Lucia" as a wakeup call.

Midnight mass audience! The first televised Christmas midnight mass was aired on TV in 1948.

How did Christmas trees become popular in America? In part, you can thank a children's book called *Kris Kringle's Christmas*. This beloved children's book of 1845 included pictures of the Christmas tree.

Charles Dickens himself read a version of the *Christmas Carol* in public. The first reading took about three hours to finish.

Irving Berlin wrote the song White Christmas and uttered that it may have been "the best song anyone has ever written." In fact, it might be. It has been recorded 500 times throughout the world and sold more than 100 million copies.

Tradition has it...

In Germany, the mother of the family
is the official tree trimmer.

Charles Dickens' *A Christmas Carol* was written, in part, to convince Victorian England about the importance of charity during the mid 1800s.

The feast of lanterns and the festival of dragons are part of the way that Christmas is celebrated in China.

Have yourself a gross little Christmas. In the 1860s, because of the Civil War, linen became scarce in the United States. A paper manufacturer in Maine decided to develop his own unique solution to the problem. He imported mummies and used the linens to make wrapping paper for gifts of the day. Talk about staying mum at Christmas.

Quick Christmas word search

Look for the words in the word search below.

```
a  t  n  a  s  s  w  o  w  s
d  e  a  r  e  r  s  n  o  w
o  y  r  t  h  c  a  t  e  d
t  o  y  s  r  i  m  r  e  c
e  f  y  u  e  n  t  l  d  f
m  u  d  d  s  o  s  o  c  e
o  r  e  e  d  n  i  e  r  e
c  o  l  s  a  n  r  k  a  r
o  f  f  m  l  f  h  t  o  t
d  y  u  l  e  d  c  u  l  e
```

Christmas   comet
reindeer   Santa
snow   tree
toys   Yule
elf   sled

Answers

```
a   t   n   a   s

                    s   n   o   w
                    a           d
t   o   y   s       m       e
e                   t   l
m                   s           e
o   r   e   e   d   n   i   e   r   e
c       l           r           r
        f           h           t
    y   u   l   e   c
```

The idea of kissing beneath mistletoe probably dates back to the 700s. In Scandinavia, the goddess Frigga, was believed to have started the tradition.

Every weekend in December, Australians take part in the "Carols By Candlelight" ceremony in different locations throughout the land down under. The idea is for people to gather at public places, such as parks, and sing carols together under the starlight.

The first Salvation Army kettle was actually a large stew pot placed outside in San Francisco in 1891. The purpose was the raise money to provide dinners for the poor of the city. The operation was a success and helped provide meals for 1,000 people. The custom spread the next year throughout the state and to Boston.

It's a hit...

What was the popular toy for 1916. None other than Lincoln Logs®, a toy that still exists today. Ironically, the toy was designed by John Wright the son of the famous architect, Frank Lloyd Wright. John was 24 when he came up with the idea.

Toys for Tots began in 1947 when a woman named Diane Hendricks made a doll for a child in need. When she asked her husband Bill, a U.S. Marine major in the reserve corp to deliver it to an agency that gave toys to kids in need, he discovered no agencies did this. So, upon Diane's advice, he and a group of marine reservists started their own unit. They delivered 5,000 toys that first year.

Austria became the first country to debut a Christmas postage stamp. It graced letters in 1937.

TV inspiration. According to legend, *The Christmas Story* was the inspiration for the TV show, *The Wonder Years*.

In 1939, Rudolph the Red Nose Reindeer joined Santa's official reindeer roster. The story was developed by Robert L. May as a way to promote the Montgomery War Department Store. Incidentally, legend has it that May originally planned to name the reindeer Reginald, but was encouraged by family members to change the name.

Figgy pudding is a real dish. Much like American bread pudding, it is a delicacy made of bread crumbs, figs, nutmeg, milk, and cinnamon. It is basked, than garnished with whipped cream, icing, or powdered sugar.

James Pierpont wrote "Jingle Bells" in 1857 as a way to commemorate the sleigh rides he watched as a little child. It was originally called "One Horse Open Sleigh." Its popularity soared in 1902, when a group called the Hayden Quartet recorded it.

Christmas jokes

1. What is Santa's favorite dog?   A pointsetter

2. How did Frosty travel? By icycle

3. How do Spanish sheep say merry Christmas?   Fleece Navidad

4. What do you call an elf comedian? A Christmas card

5. How do elves travel at the North Pole? By elfavator

6. Why should you avoid eating garland? It can give you tinselitis

7. Why did Santa plant three gardens? So he can ho-ho-ho

Good King Wenceslas was indeed a real person. However, he was not a king, he was a Bohemian duke. The Bohemians knew Wenceslas to be quite generous. However, his reign as duke lasted but five years. His brother, Boleslaw, not quite as kind, invited him to a party and then killed him.

Diamonds are a holiday's best friend. More diamonds are purchased at Christmas than any other time of the year.

Ancient Scandinavians celebrated Yule at the winter solstice. One way they celebrated – though slightly dangerous - was to put a candle wheel on top of a child's head to help represent a light on the "new wheel of the year."

Christmas trees are grown in all 50
states of the U.S, even Hawaii.

The Christmas Song, aka "Chestnuts Roasting On an Open Fire" was written by Mel Torme and Robert Wells. The duo penned the song in about 45 minutes and did it in the middle of a heat wave in 1945.

More Reindeer Facts

1. Caribou and reindeer are the same animal. In North America, they are known as caribou and in Europe, they are called reindeer.

2. Laplanders began to domesticate the animal 3,000 years ago.

3. Reindeer have been raised for their milk.

4. Most reindeer in Europe and Asia have been domesticated.

5. In North America, large herds of wild caribou roam free. When the Alaska Pipeline was built, the design had to take into account that caribou roam wild in the pipeline region.

It's a hit...

What was the hit toy for all kids in 1979? Well, none other than the beloved Rubik's Cube ®, one of the most iconic Christmas gifts of all time. It was so popular, even adults wanted it.

The Christmas present rush began as a concept in the early 1940s. At the time, people had to purchase presents earlier in the season to get them overseas for soldiers fighting in World War II. Even after the war ended, the rush had become part of the holiday way of life. It remains to this day, as a remnant from World War II.

The first White House postcards were sent in 1953. Then president Dwight D. Eisenhower sent out 2,000 of the cards to his closest buddies.

Bing Crosby recorded the most beloved song, *White Christmas* in 1942. To this day, nearly everyone has come to love the favorite song. Everyone that is, except Bing himself. It took him only 18 minutes to record it and he was not impressed with how it sounded. However, at the time, he was not able to re-record it. Good thing. It is the best selling Christmas song of all time.

The most popular type of Christmas trees are Scotch pine and Douglas fir. The girth, height, and feel of the needles, as well as the scent, make these popular trees.

It's a hit...

The popular gift of 1949 for kids was a gift fitting for the holiday. That year, kids were clamoring to get the board game *Candyland®*.

The Worcester Wreath Company of Maine started placing wreaths on the graves of veterans at Arlington National Cemetery. They started the custom in 1992 and each year, volunteers from the company take 5000 wreaths and place them on graves at the cemetery.

Charlie Brown may have been one of the most famous figures to bemoan the commercialization of Christmas in the 1965 classic *A Charlie Brown Christmas.* However, Harriet Beecher Stowe helped introduce the idea of a character railing against the commercialization of the holiday a century earlier in her 1850s story "The First Christmas in New England."

Santa Paws. About 70 percent of people include their own pets in the "gift getting" experience at Christmas. They make sure that Santa Paws leaves a good gift.

No one knows for sure, but some professors believe Ebenezer Scrooge may have been based on a real person. According to Sjef de Jong, a Dutch scholar, Dickens may have been inspired to invent Scrooge while learning about a Dutch grave digger named Gabriel de Graaf, who lived in the 1800s. The real life man known for being rather cantankerous supposedly disappeared on Christmas Eve one night and reappeared later a much kinder and friendlier man. According to Graaf, a band of dwarves kidnapped and made him a changed man. As a side note, supposedly, Graaf also drank a lot, too.

Boxing Day is the name given to the day after Christmas. It is celebrated in many of the former British territories, including Canada and Australia. The day gets it name from the fact that people broke down boxes on the day after all gifts had been open. In Australia, the day is celebrated with many sporting events, such as the Sydney to Hobart Yacht Race.

When Queen Victoria married Prince Albert in 1840, the custom of celebrating Christmas took off. Albert, from Germany, brought the customs of celebrating the holiday from his native Germany. Soon, people all over Victorian England were celebrating the holiday.

Three Wise Men? The Bible does not actually tell how many wise men showed up at Christ's birthplace. Tradition has turned it in to three wise men. Often, they are depicted as men representing the three stages of adult hood – a young adult, a middle age man, and old man. Incidentally, they are often referred to as Magi, which is the root word in "magician." This means "wise one."

What's the busiest shopping day of the year? Black Friday you say? Nay. The Friday after Thanksgiving ranks in the top five (it is often four or five on a given year). However, typically, the busiest shopping day is the Saturday before Christmas, when people are doing their last minute scramble. Avoid the malls that day.

Christmas by the numbers.....

1 = one star seen over Bethlehem

2 = two books of the Bible that have the Christmas Story (Mark and Luke)

3 = three wise men that show up at the birth of Jesus

4 = four words in the French word Noel

5 = five points of a Christmas star

6 = six sides of a snowflake falling on Christmas Day

7 = seven continents Santa visits on Christmas Eve

8 = eight original reindeer Santa had

9 = nine reindeer Santa now uses

10 = ten years old is how old Christmas trees should be before cut.

Bah humbug! This most famous Dicken's line actually began as Bah Christmas. However, Dickens realized the line needed a little retouching and changed it.

www.ingramcontent.com/pod-product-compliance
Lightning Source LLC
Chambersburg PA
CBHW081831280526
45789CB00007B/2426